LIBERATION

A 30-Day Devotional For Men in Prison

Thirty Days' Journey to Discover Jesús, and Let Him Be the Center of Your Heart to Set You Free

Annett Hill

Now the Lord is that Spirit: and where the Spirit of the Lord is, there is liberty.
2 Corinthians 3:17

TABLE OF CONTENTS

How to Use This Devotional

This book should help you learn what God has to say about thirty daily concerns that many of us struggle with. Avoid cramming in too much studying at once. One passage should serve as a solid foundation, rather than rushing through others without gaining anything.

It should help you change your life, which will provide peace of mind and comfort despite any challenges you may be currently experiencing.

Finding a quiet area and having a pen or pencil on hand can help you make the most of this devotional. You need a Bible, so that you can study it and learn to know God's word for yourself. You must also learn the scriptures, especially the ones that speak to you personally.

I advise you to use this devotional with an open mind, so you can learn new things and God will communicate with you through this book.

I created this devotional with interaction in mind. You can fill up the blanks provided to write the responses to the targeted questions. Beyond that, though, feel free to jot down your views as you read the book and analyze it.

Finally, as you study try to answer the following questions

1. *What is God trying to say to me? What new thing have I learned today that I will apply?*
2. *What adjustments do I need to make in my relationship with God and my fellow man?*
3. *Write out things you will need to pray about.*

INTRODUCTION

"You can chain me, you can torture me, you can even destroy this body, but you will never imprison my mind." Mahatma Gandhi, Father of Modern India.

"And you shall know the truth, and the truth shall make you free." John 8:32.

In 1994, the movie "The Shawshank Redemption" starring Tim Robbins and Morgan Freeman, though not a box office success, became one of the most highly rated movies of that decade. It was the story of a man jailed for allegedly killing his wife and her lover, and sentenced to life imprisonment (a crime he didn't do). His illustrious career as an accountant and life ended abruptly.

However, the movie portrays the victory of the mind over chains and pains. It showed that if a man's mind is free, no matter what is done to cage him, he will always rise above injustice, brutality, and oppression. When your mind is free, then anything is possible!

One of the greatest things God has given you is your mind, and you can accomplish everything your mind can conjure up. What you feed your mind now will determine what it produces for you tomorrow. You may feel the serenity and tranquility God wants in your soul and spirit by using your mind to transcend the bars of the jail, the hate, rage, violence, death, and extremely negative energies around you.

This devotional helps you use tried-and-true Biblical concepts over 30 days, which will help you overcome many of the difficulties associated with serving time. This devotional will also help you learn Bible texts that encourage you to persevere and stay focused, as well as help you jot down your ideas while you study. To strengthen your faith, I advise you to memorize 30 verses over 30 days.

The truth of God's Word has the power to liberate your mind and conscience and make you free.

Shalom.

Topic: Feeling Unloved?
Central Truth: JESUS LOVES YOU!

> *"I have told you this so that my joy may be in you and that your joy may be complete. My command is this: Love each other as I have loved you. Greater love has no one than this: to lay down one's life for one's friends. You are my friends if you do what I command. I no longer call you servants because a servant does not know his master's business. Instead, I have called you friends, for everything that I learned from my Father I have made known to you. You did not choose me, but I chose you and appointed you so that you might go and bear fruit—fruit that will last— and so that whatever you ask in my name, the Father will give you".*
> *John 15:11-16 (NIV).*

In Greek culture, the word "love" has five distinct meanings: "Philia," friendship love; "Storge," a familiar love, such as that between a mother and child or a sibling; "Eros," a sensual love; and "personal love." Other names for love are "Philautia," self-love, and "Agape," an unchanging, unconditional love.

The Greek word agape, which means "unconditional love," is the love used in the Bible to describe God's love for us. Imagine for a moment that you are alone and waiting for an event to start, when someone sits down next to you and starts talking. Even if you didn't ask for it or deserve it, that person attempted to show you they were concerned about you. That is the degree to which Jesus loves you.

You and I don't qualify to be loved. We all have made mistakes and probably will make some more, but Jesus doesn't look at us by what we have done, but by what he has done, and he wants to walk up to you, sit by you, take you by the hand, and care for you. He wants to clean the slate of your past life and give you another chance to start again.

So, why will Jesus love you despite all you may have done? The answer is in his nature.

1 John 4:8 says God is love, and he came as a man to pay for the sins of mankind because he loves us. It was his choice, and if you were the only one on earth, Jesus would still have come and died for you.

The crucifixion is a striking illustration of the good news that "God is for us", as stated in Romans 8:32. The atoning death of the Savior is evidence of God's love. Will you not ask the Lord to help you remove anything obstructing the flow of His unwavering love? God is love, and He showed us this by sending His Son to die "while we were still sinners" (Romans 5:8).

God loves you. In the Bible, he frequently states this. Believe nothing I say. See for yourself how much He cares by reading His Word. (1 John 4:9-21). God loves you with everlasting love, and he will never give up on you. When you call, he will always be available.

Questions:
Why did Jesus say he loves me?
1..
2..
What type of love does the Bible say Jesus has for me? (tick the right box)
1. Conditional ■   Unconditional ■
2. Selfless ■   Selfish ■
3. Philia ■   Storge ■   Agape ■
What do I do when I feel so unloved?
1..
2..
What changes will you make today because of this study?
1..
2..
3..

Personal Notes: Write whatever the Spirit of God lays in your heart and pray about it

....
....
....
....
....
....
....
....
....
....
....
....
....
....
....
....
....
....
....
....
....
....
....
....

Assignment: Memorize John 15:13.
Bravo, you have completed Day 1. Now tick yourself a Pass ▊

Today's Prayer

Lord Teach me to:

Today I am grateful for:

Topic: Want to be free?
Central Truth: YOU CAN BE FREE.

> *"Therefore, there is now no condemnation for those who are in Christ Jesus, because through Christ Jesus the law of the Spirit who gives life has set you free from the law of sin and death. For what the law was powerless to do because it was weakened by the flesh, God did by sending his own Son in the likeness of sinful flesh to be a sin offering. And so he condemned sin in the flesh. In order that the righteous requirement of the law might be fully met in us, who do not live according to the flesh but according to the Spirit. "Romans 8:1-4.*
>
> *"So Christ has truly set us free. Now make sure that you stay free, and don't get tied up again in slavery to the law." Galatians 5:1 (NLT)*

The Oxford English Dictionary defines freedom as the power or right to act, speak, or think as one wants without hindrance or restraint. It is the state of not being imprisoned or enslaved. The opposite of freedom is slavery.

Despite being physically free, social vices, poverty, injustice, terror, habits, and addictions constrain many people. Many prisoners have greater freedom than those outside of prison. Because of your addictions and guilt, your heart and mind may seem like they are dead, yet God can bring you back to life. God's Son took the punishment we deserved. What a gift!

This shows that there are certain freedoms that neither the state nor the government can grant you. One can be in bondage without being imprisoned. You and I can start a new life when we accept God's free invitation to be saved. Maybe you have experienced what it's like to feel betrayed, despised, and looked down upon by the world like Jesus did.

Real freedom comes from knowing God and his word and having a relationship with him through his son, Jesus Christ. It is only Jesus that can set you free!

Those who accept that gift will never have to face the sting of God's rejection. All you must do is accept the deal being offered to you. You may feel that you're so far off course that God could never find you.

But God knew you by your name before you were born. And long ago, He set the plan in motion to rescue you and turn your life around again. The offer is on the table. Now it's up to you.

Questions:

What is real freedom, according to today's lesson?

1..

2..

What does the Bible say my freedom will come from? Answer Yes or No.

1. From the Declaration of Independence. Yes ■ No ■

2. From a relationship with God through Jesus Christ. Yes ■ No ■

What are the things you need to do to exercise true freedom? Choose one option.

1.. firm in the word of God. (Sleep, Stand, Slip)

2 All you must do is.................................. the deal being offered to you. (Accept, Reject, Forget)

3 Live according to the.................................. (Flesh, Spirit, State)

What changes will you make today because of this study?

1..

2..

3..

Personal Notes: Write whatever the Spirit of God lays in your heart and pray about it

....
....
....
....
....
....
....
....
....
....
....
....
....
....
....
....
....
....
....
....
....
....
....
....

Assignment: Memorize Philippians 4:4.
Bravo, you have completed Day 2. Now tick yourself a Pass ▇

Today's Prayer

Lord Teach me to:

Today I am grateful for:

Topic: Feeling Unforgiven?
Theme: GOD WILL FORGIVE YOU.

> *"Come now, let us settle the matter," says the LORD. "Though your sins are like scarlet, they shall be as white as snow; though they are red as crimson, they shall be like wool." Isaiah 1:18*
>
> *"And forgive us our debts, as we also have forgiven our debtors." Matthew 6:12*

No man on earth doesn't need to forgive or be forgiven. In our daily lives, we offend people and get offended ourselves. No man is infallible, and there is no man without a past.

In the book of John 8:3-11, there is the story of a woman who was "caught in adultery" and brought to Jesus to see what his verdict would be. According to the Law of Moses, she was to be stoned to death, for they caught her in the act. Jesus, knowing the hypocrisy of men, looked at them and said nothing, writing with his finger on the ground.

Now, the man who committed adultery with her was let off the hook, but they brought her forward to be killed. Jesus after a while looked up and said, "He who has no sin let him cast the first stone". They all left one after the other, from the oldest to the youngest, because before God, we are all guilty.

The gospel is for the lost, because you need a Savior, and God justifies the ungodly as you. The sinner is the gospel reason for existence, and Jesus Christ came to the world to forgive sinners.

What he has done is to provide a remedy for your sins and ensure that his son Jesus Christ paid the penalty, so that you may be free.

It is like you have a speeding ticket and someone pays your fine for you. You will no longer be required to pay anything, will you?

Breaking the law not only offends people and the government, but also violates God's commandments, making us guilty in God's eyes.

On the cross of Calvary, Jesus paid it all and said, "It is finished"; PAID IN FULL with his precious blood. What you must do is accept the sacrifice of Jesus, confess that you have wronged, that you are sorry, and ask Him to forgive you.

God wants you to ask for forgiveness, even though he knows of your transgressions. If you do, He will pardon all of them. God can change you; you shouldn't want to recall things that God has already elected to forget. I will not remember your sins. (Hebrews 8:12).

You will also need to forgive yourself and others who may have hurt you, because YOU ARE FORGIVEN!

Questions:
Why do we all need to be forgiven?
1...
2...
What does the Bible say about forgiveness? Answer Yes or No
1. I have sinned against God and man when I break the law.
    Yes ▆▆ No ▆▆
2. I am forgiven as I forgive others
    Yes ▆▆ No. ▆▆
What are the things you need to do to be forgiven?
1. Admit that you have.. against God.
2. .... your sins
3. Ask him to.. you.

What changes will you make today because of this study?

1...

2...

3...

Personal Notes: Write whatever the Spirit of God lays in your heart, and pray about it

....

....

....

....

....

....

....

....

....

....

....

....

....

....

....

....

....

Assignment: Memorize Isaiah 1:18.

Bravo, you have completed Day 3. Now tick yourself a Pass

Today's Prayer

Lord Teach me to:

Today I am grateful for:

Topic: Feeling Rejected?
Central Truth: GOD ACCEPTS YOU JUST AS YOU ARE.

> *"Jephthah the Gileadite was a mighty warrior. His father was Gilead; his mother was a prostitute. Gilead's wife also bore him sons, and when they were grown up, they drove Jephthah away. "You are not going to get any inheritance in our family," they said, "because you are the son of another woman." So, Jephthah fled from his brothers and settled in the land of Tob, where a gang of scoundrels gathered around him and followed him. Sometime later, when the Ammonites were fighting against Israel, the elders of Gilead went to get Jephthah from the land of Tob. "Come," they said, "be our commander, so we can fight the Ammonites." Jephthah said to them, "Didn't you hate me and drive me from my father's house? Why do you come to me now when you're in trouble?" The elders of Gilead said to him, "Nevertheless, we are turning to you now; come with us to fight the Ammonites, and you will be head over all of us who live in Gilead."*
> *Judges 11:1-8*

Psychologists will tell you that one reason people develop depressive disorders and unhealthy habits is rejection. According to Pastor Derek Prince, even unborn children can feel rejected, and this could impact their mental health.

In today's scripture, Jephthah, the firstborn son of Gilead, who was born to a prostitute, was expelled from his inheritance by his brothers. He suffered from being labeled an illegitimate kid, rejection from his parents, abandonment by his mother, and expulsion from his siblings.

Despite all the difficulties, Jephthah didn't give up or let depression engulf him. Instead, he moved from the place of rejection to the land of Tob, where he was not only welcomed but also saw the manifestation of his gifts.

Do not be concerned when people reject you because they believe you are not brilliant, attractive, or good enough. God still has hope for you. Know that God wants you even if your spouse leaves you, your mother abandoned you at birth, or she put you up for adoption because she didn't want you.

In Psalm 139:14, David said, "I will worship you because I am wonderfully and fearfully made." Jephthah understood that his destiny was dependent not on what others thought of him, but on his perception of himself and what would happen to him. Those who originally rejected him eventually made him their leader and commander. That's going to be your story!

Questions:

Why is rejection something that we need to deal with? Answer Yes or No

1. It can lead to a state of low self-esteem. Yes ▮ No ▮
2. It can lead to depression and suicidal tendencies. Yes ▮ No. ▮

What did Jephthah do when he faced rejection from his family?

1. He.............................. Gilead for the land of.................................
2. He began to.. his skills and became a
    champion warrior
3. He was............................ (Furious, fuming and angry, focused).
    Choose one option!

Why did Jephthah not allow rejection depressed him?

1. What people think about you is not as important
as..
....
2. He knew he was................................ and..
made by God.

Remember, when people reject you, God accepts you.

The secret to freedom is to believe what God says about you, regardless of what others have said about you. If God is for you, as stated in Romans 8:31, who can be against you? God accepts you because of who God is, not because of who you are. Remember that God loves you unconditionally; when you accept this, your life will be transformed. Trust what God says about you right now, and choose restoration.

What changes will you make today because of this study?

1..

2..

3..

Personal Notes: Write whatever the Spirit of God lays in your heart, and pray about it

....

....

....

....

....

....

....

....

....

....

....

....

....

....

....

....

....

Assignment: Memorize Psalms 139:14.

Bravo, you have completed Day 4. Now tick yourself a Pass

Today's Prayer

Lord Teach me to:

Today I am grateful for:

Topic: Betrayed? (Backstabbed)
Central Theme: YOU CAN TRUST JESUS TOTALLY.

> *"And while they were reclining and eating, Jesus said, "Truly I tell you, one of you who is eating with Me will betray Me." Mark 14:18*

> *"While He was still speaking, behold, Judas, one of the twelve, came up accompanied by a large crowd with swords and clubs, who came from the chief priests and elders of the people. Now he who was betraying Him gave them a sign, saying, "Whomever I kiss, He is the one; seize Him." Immediately Judas went to Jesus and said, "Hail, Rabbi!" and kissed Him. And Jesus said to him, "Friend, do what you have come for." Then they came and laid hands-on Jesus and seized Him."*
> *Matthew 26:47-50*

In the famous Shakespeare play "Julius Caesar," Brutus, Julius Caesar's close friend, betrays him. When Julius Caesar looks to him for help, Brutus plunges his knife and kills his comrade. Julius Caesar, in his dying moment, turned to his buddy and said, "And You Brutus," expressing his grief at being stabbed in the back by someone whom he trusted with his life.

Don't allow bitterness and anger to block the beauty from relating to people. Being close to people involves a certain level of risk, because you are vulnerable to being hurt by those you love. If you have been backstabbed, so have millions of people, so your case is not isolated. Backstabbing by friends and loved ones is as old as history itself.

It's like saying you'll never get into a car again, since automobile accidents cause deaths! People still buy vehicles, despite the possibility of fatalities in auto accidents. Relationships are like that.

One of Jesus' trusted disciples, Judas, betrayed him. He remained loyal to him, despite knowing in advance that he would turn on him. It is living a life of self-denial to claim that I don't want to be betrayed. Even if you may experience betrayal in the future, you must persevere, just like Jesus did.

Backstabbing makes us lose trust in people, but you can put your trust in Jesus. He is a reliable friend that will never betray you. He says, "I will never leave you nor forsake you".

Jesus got your back covered!

Questions:

Why is it that those close to us betray us?
1. Because in every relationship you are...
(protected, vulnerable, ignored) Choose the best option.
2. It is those closest to us that know our.....................................
(weapons, power, secrets) Choose the best option.

Is it possible never to be betrayed in life?
Yes ▮ No ▮ (Think about this before you tick an option)

Should you stop relating to people because of betrayal?
Yes. ▮ No. ▮ (Tick one option)

Why should you trust Jesus?
1. He is...
2. He will never.................................. you nor................................. you.
3. He got your.. covered.

What changes will you make today because of this study?

1..

2..

3..

Personal Notes: Write whatever the Spirit of God lays in your heart, and pray about it

....
....
....
....
....
....
....
....
....
....
....
....
....
....
....
....
....
....
....

Assignment: Memorize Psalms 28:3.

Bravo, you have completed Day 5. Now tick yourself a Pass ▨

Today's Prayer

Lord Teach me to:

Today I am grateful for:

Topic: Feeling unworthy?
Central truth: YOU ARE WORTHY IN GOD'S EYES.

> *"When the angel of the LORD came and sat down under the oak in Ophrah that belonged to Joash the Abiezrite, where his son Gideon was threshing wheat in a winepress to hide it from the Midianites. And the angel of the LORD appeared to Gideon and said, "The LORD is with you, O mighty man of valor." "Please, my Lord," Gideon replied, "if the LORD is with us, why has all this happened to us? And where are all His wonders of which our fathers told us, saying, 'Has, not the LORD brought us up out of Egypt?' But now the LORD has forsaken us and delivered us into the hand of Midian." The LORD turned to him and said, "Go in the strength you have and save Israel from the hand of Midian. Am I not sending you?" "Please, my Lord," Gideon replied, "how can I save Israel? Indeed, my clan is the weakest in Manasseh, and I am the youngest in my father's house." "Surely I will be with you," the LORD replied, "and you will strike down all the Midianites as one man." Judges 6:11-16*

One obstacle preventing people from being the finest versions of themselves God intended is low self-esteem. Many factors can cause low self-esteem, including one's upbringing, family traditions, media messages, verbal and physical abuse as a kid, failure at things others excel at, and fear (real or perceived).

The late Dr. Myles Munroe was reportedly referred to as a dullard and incapable of learning by his English teacher. He became the top graduating student and well-known preacher, evangelist, and motivational speaker thanks to his mother's support, who handed him the Bible to study and memorize.

In today's chapter, God saw Gideon as a powerful man, yet he was hiding.

The angel informed him he would free Israel from its adversaries, but his self-evaluation revealed a lack of self-worth. He said that by being the youngest member of his father's household and the weakest member of his tribe, he was ineligible for whatever God was planning to do. According to his opinion, he didn't have what it took to succeed. The circumstances shaped his idea of him, but God doesn't operate with human opinions.

We all feel unworthy at different points in our lives. Adam and Eve felt unworthy when God promised a Savior who would come and save them from their sins. The Apostle Paul felt unworthy when Jesus stopped him on the road to Damascus one day when he was still Saul. Peter felt unworthy after he denied Jesus three times, but he entrusted him with his flocks.

Only you can fulfill the purpose for which God gave you life. God is counting on you to be successful in a field that only you are a master at. But nothing meaningful can ever be achieved if you keep believing the lies of the devil. He wants you to believe that you are unprepared for success and lack the information, resources, connections, and skills required.

According to a once said phrase, extraordinary people are ordinary people doing extraordinary things. Confess what God says about you every day, and see yourself rise above every limitation.

Questions
List three major things that make people feel unworthy or have low self-esteem.

1..
2..
3..

Why is our opinion about ourselves sometimes incorrect?
1. Because we cannot.................................. ourselves as God knows us (love, know, value). Choose one option.
2. Because our..................................... do not depend on what we say or what people say (Worth, Reputation, Business) Choose one option.

Name one important key to your success. Choose from the options below:
1. Hiding from our enemies. ▮
2. Comparing ourselves with other people around us. ▮
3. Confessing what God says about us daily. ▮

What changes will you make today because of this study?
1..
2..
3..

Personal Notes: Write whatever the Spirit of God lays in your heart, and pray about it

....
....
....
....
....
....
....
....
....
....

Assignment: Memorize Philippians 4:13.
Bravo, you have completed Day 6. Now tick yourself a Pass ▮

Today's Prayer

Lord Teach me to:

Today I am grateful for:

Topic: Lacking faith?
Central Theme: JESUS WANTS TO TEACH YOU HOW TO WALK BY FAITH.

> *During the fourth watch of the night, Jesus went out to them, walking on the sea. When the disciples saw Him walking on the sea, they were terrified. "It's a ghost!" they said and cried out in fear. But Jesus spoke up at once: "Take courage! It is I. Do not be afraid." "Lord, if it is You," Peter replied, "command me to come to You on the water." "Come," said Jesus. Then Peter got down out of the boat, walked on the water, and came toward Jesus. But when he saw the strength of the wind, he was afraid, and beginning to sink, cried out, "Lord, save me!" Immediately Jesus reached out His hand and took hold of Peter. "You of little faith," He said, "why did you doubt?" Matthew 14:25-31*
>
> *"The Lord answered, "If you had faith even as small as a mustard seed, you could say to this mulberry tree, 'May you be uprooted and planted in the sea,' and it would obey you!" Luke 17:6*

Faith is the currency with which spiritual transactions with God are done, and as Christians, we cannot do without faith. Faith is our purchasing power in the spirit realm, and we need to live a life of Christ-giving service in all things.

Jesus walked on water to get to his disciples and when Peter saw him, he asked him to invite him to walk on water as well. When he removed his eyes from Jesus and saw the wind, he began to sink. Jesus grabbed Peter, restored him, and asked why he doubted.

Faith is trusting God no matter what you're experiencing, knowing that he has your best interest at heart. To trust God is to have confidence in him and his word. You may not need to walk on water, but God wants us to live by faith.

To trust God is to have confidence in him and his word. You must believe it is possible before it happens. Hebrews 11:1.

One thing about faith is that it does not come naturally. It must be activated, cultivated, and grown. The good news is that there is a bit of faith in all believers, and if you put your faith to work, no matter how small, it can yield great testimonies for you. Obeying God when you do not understand it. Hebrew 11:7 demonstrates this.

Jesus told Peter that all that was needed to walk on water (do the supernatural) was not to doubt. He was not rebuked for having small faith, but rebuked for doubting that his small faith can bring a big miracle.

Ignite your faith. Trust God for the small things, and as you grow, you will trust God for the bigger things, and your life will be a testimony of supernatural encounters. The place to start is by reading and studying the word of God, because faith comes from hearing and hearing the word of God. (Romans 10:17)

That is what God desires for you.

Questions

How can you define faith?
1. Faith is.................................. God (Praying to, Worshiping, trusting). Choose one option.
What did the Bible say in Luke 17:6 that a little faith can do? Choose one option.
1. Little faith can do mighty.................................. (Farming, agriculture, miracles)
2. Little faith can do what looks.. (Impossible, immovable, untouchable)

How do we ignite our faith?

1..
2..
3..

What changes will you make today because of this study?

1..
2..
3..

Personal Notes: Write whatever the Spirit of God lays in your heart, and pray about it

....
....
....
....
....
....
....
....
....
....
....
....
....
....
....
....
....
....
....

Assignment: Memorize Romans 10:17.

Bravo, you have completed Day 7. Now tick yourself a Pass ▮

Today's Prayer

Lord Teach me to:

Today I am grateful for:

Topic: Are you cursed?
Central truth: JESUS DIED SO YOU CAN BE BLESSED.

> *"God is not human, that he should lie, not a human being, that he should change his mind. Does he speak and then not act? Does he promise and not fulfill? I have received a command to bless; he has blessed, and I cannot change it. "No misfortune is seen in Jacob, no misery observed in Israel. The Lord their God is with them; the shout of the King is among them. God brought them out of Egypt; they have the strength of a wild ox. "There is no divination against Jacob, no evil omens against Israel. It will now be said of Jacob and of Israel, 'See what God has done!' The people rise like a lioness; they rouse themselves like a lion that does not rest till it devours its prey and drinks the blood of its victims." Numbers 23:19-24.*

> *"Christ redeemed us from the curse of the law by becoming a curse for us, for it is written: "Cursed is everyone who is hung on a pole." He redeemed us in order that the blessing given to Abraham might come to the Gentiles through Christ Jesus, so that by faith we might receive the promise of the Spirit. Galatians 3:13-14*

Curses are real and can affect people from generation to generation. How do you explain a family where no male child ever reaches the age of 45? They all die in their early 40s or before. I know one family where virtually every member of that family has done time in jail.

This can appear a coincidence, but when it develops into a trend within a family, it becomes a cause of concern.

The first thing to mention about curses is that the entire human race is under the original curse. That is the curse God imposed on the planet as punishment for Adam and Eve and our sins.

Aside from the curse of God, we may also be susceptible to our curses and the curses of those who desire to ruin our destiny. One way they work is by passing on a curse from parent to child.

A curse is like an invisible hand that hovers over someone and ensures nothing good happens to them. As soon as one is about to break through, something goes wrong, and you are back to square one.

The good news is that Christ can free us from the shackles of curses, because one of the main reasons He came was to do this. He has purchased our freedom from the curse of the law, according to Galatians. Because of our acts of omission and commission, some spiritual laws are set up to operate against us. Yet the blood of Jesus can remove every curse from our lives and give us a brand new beginning.

When things are not just working for you despite your best efforts, you need to submit to Jesus Christ, who wants you to live a life of abundance. (John 10:10).

Questions:
Why does the Bible say all men are under a curse?
1. It is because our ancestors........................ and.. sinned against God.
2. Curses can be.................................... from generation to generation.

How do you identify a curse at work in your life?
1. When things are not.. despite your best...
2. When you are disaster or accident prone.
Why are curses very serious?
1. Curses can.................................... you from fulfilling your destiny (promote, announce, hinder) choose one option

2. A curse if like an ....destructive hand (visible, invisible, cloudy)

How do we deal with curses?

1. Know that as a child of God, you are..............................and no one can..............................you

2. Know that God has....................................to bless you, and he will not change his mind

3. Meditate on Galatians 3:13-14 and personalize it

What changes will you make today because of this study?

1...

2...

3...

Personal Notes: Write whatever the Spirit of God lays in your heart, and pray about it

....
....
....
....
....
....
....
....
....
....
....
....
....
....
....
....

Assignment: Memorize Galatians 3:13-14.

Bravo, you have completed Day 8. Now tick yourself a Pass ▨

Today's Prayer

Lord Teach me to:

Today I am grateful for:

Topic: Are you sick?
Central Theme: GOD WANTS TO HEAL YOU.

"Then a leper came to Jesus, begging on his knees: "If You are willing, you can make me clean." Moved with compassion, Jesus reached out His hand and touched the man. "I am willing," He said. "Be clean!" And immediately the leprosy left him, and the man was cleansed." *Mark 1:40-41*

"Jesus went throughout Galilee, teaching in their synagogues, proclaiming the good news of the kingdom, and healing every disease and sickness among the people." Matthew 4:23

People often ask why God would allow sickness to exist if he is a loving God. No one is immune from sickness. Just remember the devastating effects of the COVID-19 pandemic, which killed over 2 million people worldwide, and the devastating effect it had on the world economy.

The answer is that sickness is one wage (payment) we received because of Adam and Eve's sin. God's original intention for us was for our minds to be sound, but because of the fall of man, sin has exposed us to disease, death, and all the other tragedies of a fallen world.

I am not saying if you are sick; it is because you have sinned. Although, it is good to examine if the sickness results from carelessness or abuse of your body. Otherwise, know that God may not stop you from being sick. He will bring healing and break the yoke of sickness over you.

Throughout the Bible, and even up till now, people are getting healed from all forms of sickness; cancer, diabetes, hypertension, heart diseases, bone diseases, and many more. The power of God is still at work, and he will continue to deliver those who believe in him.

Don't give up if you are struggling with your health. Jesus continues to provide divine healing. The songwriter brilliantly captures it.

> *"The great Physician now is here,*
> *the sympathizing Jesus*
> *He speaks the drooping heart to cheer.*
> *Oh, hear the name of Jesus!*
>
> *Sweetest note in seraph song*
> *Sweetest name on mortal tongue*
> *Sweetest carol ever song*
> *Jesus blessed Jesus.*

Isaiah 53:5 says by his stripes, we were healed. They beat Jesus with 39 stripes torture called halfway death. After the process, he was barely recognizable, and he did it all because of you.

Your healing has been secured; all you need to do is claim it!

Questions
Why, according to John 9:1-2, do people fall sick sometimes?
Answer yes or no
1. They have committed sin. Yes ■ No ■
2. Their parents are sinners. Yes ■ No ■
3. God wants to be glorified by healing them. Yes ■ No ■

When sickness knocks, what are we to do? Choose one option.
1. We are........................ panic. (Continue to; not to; be indifferent to)
2. Take the matter up with God in......................... (Complaining, crying, prayers)
3. Claim what the.. says about your health. (Doctors; People; Bible)

4. Trust in God... (Absolutely; Occasionally; Temporarily)

Keep in mind that the devil will try to convince you that you will perish from your illness, or that God is unable or unwilling to heal you. That is an evil lie straight out of hell. Jeremiah 30:17 states God will give you back your health and heal your wounds. Though the doctors may make the diagnosis accurate, God alone determines the ultimate result.

Pray this prayer repeatedly:
"Father in heaven, I thank you, because you are not a man to lie. You have said that by the stripes that Jesus, your son, and my Savior took, I am healed. Therefore, Lord God, I claim my healing over... (mention the sickness) and declare that I am healed and completely made whole in Jesus' mighty name.

What changes will you make today because of this study?
1...
2...
3...

Personal Notes: Write whatever the Spirit of God lays in your heart, and pray about it
....
....
....
....
....
....

Assignment: Memorize. Isaiah 53:5; Matthew 8:7; 1 Peter 2:24
Bravo, you have completed Day 9. Now tick yourself a Pass ■

Today's Prayer

Lord Teach me to:

Today I am grateful for:

Topic: Are you oppressed?
Central truth: YOU CAN BE DELIVERED FROM OPPRESSION.

> *"The LORD said, "I have surely seen the affliction of My people who are in Egypt, and have given heed to their cry because of their taskmasters, for I am aware of their sufferings. "So, I have come down to deliver them from the power of the Egyptians, and to bring them up from that land to a good and spacious land, to a land flowing with milk and honey, to the place of the Canaanite and the Hittite and the Amorite and the Perizzite and the Hivite and the Jebusite. Exodus 3:7-9*
>
> *"Again, I looked and saw all the oppression that was taking place under the sun: I saw the tears of the oppressed and they have no comforter; power was on the side of their oppressors and they have no comforter."*
> *Ecclesiastes 4:1.*

Oppression is prolonged cruel or unjust treatment or control, often under the guise of governmental authority or cultural opprobrium. The state of being subject to unjust treatment or control is one of the most serious forms of oppression.

According to the verses above, God detests oppression and always takes action to stop it. God sent Moses to deliver his people from the Egyptians, who had oppressed them and turned them into slaves.

The Egyptians were cruel to the Israelites and subjected them to rigorous hard labor. Moses did great signs and wonders and broke the power of Pharaoh before he released God's people.

Because the oppressor has control over you, your life, and what you can do, oppression is equivalent to slavery.

The Bible considers oppression wickedness, since the victim receives no comfort from the oppressor's actions.

Has someone more powerful or connected than you exploited you or denied you anything that was rightfully yours? Have you experienced injustice because people thought you couldn't stand up for yourself?

Whatever the case, God detests oppression, but he can only defend the oppressed when they call him for help. You cannot get help through the country's judicial system, but everyone who trusts in God can receive God's justice.

Vindicate me, oh Lord, should be your heart cry!

Questions:
Why is it that people can oppress others? Choose one option.
1, They occupy.. positions
(government; privileged; honorable)
2. They have................................. on their side. (Power; Money; People)
3. When you don't........................... your right (accept; know; discuss)

Why is the oppressor advantageous?
1. No one can challenge him/her.   Yes ■   No ■
2. He/she has power on his/her side.   Yes ■   No ■
3. The oppressed have no one to comfort them. Yes ■   No. ■

Who should start your deliverance from oppression?
1. God Almighty?   Yes ■   No ■
2. Your Pastor?   Yes ■   No ■
3. Yourself?   Yes ■   No ■

What changes will you make today because of this study?

1...

2...

3...

Personal Notes: Write whatever the Spirit of God lays in your heart, and pray about it

....

....

....

....

....

....

....

....

....

....

....

....

....

....

....

....

....

....

Assignment: Memorize. Ecclesiastes 4:1

Bravo, you have completed Day 10. Now tick yourself a Pass ▪

Today's Prayer

_____
_____
_____
_____
_____
_____
_____
_____
_____

Lord Teach me to:

_____
_____
_____
_____
_____
_____
_____
_____
_____
_____

Today I am grateful for:

_____
_____
_____
_____
_____
_____
_____
_____
_____
_____

Topic: Feeling unredeemable?
Central truth: JESUS WILL REDEEM YOU.

> *"For I brought you out of Egypt and redeemed you from slavery. I sent Moses, Aaron, and Miriam to help you." Micah 6:4*
>
> *"Turn to me and have mercy, for I am alone and in deep distress. My problems go from bad to worse. Oh, save me from them all! Feel my pain and see my trouble. Forgive all my sins. See how many enemies I have and how viciously they hate me! Protect me! Rescue my life from them! Do not let me be disgraced, for in you I take refuge. May integrity and honesty protect me, for I put my hope in you. O God, ransom Israel from all its troubles." Psalms 25:16-22*

Imagine you lost a precious watch given to you by your father. One day, you walk into a pawnshop and find it sitting on their shelf on display with a price tag. Because of the emotional attachment you have to the watch, you decide to buy it back - even though it was originally yours.

God created you in His image and likeness, and you carry the stamp of his ownership, but sins and the choices we make lead us to the part of being lost. Therefore, he sent his son Jesus to pay the ransom fee to buy you back. This is the wonderful story of God's redemption.

Regardless of what you've done or how lost you are, God has already made plans for your restoration. You need a second chance, just like everyone else, since Christ died before you were ever born. God gives everyone a second chance to make things right, which is the most beautiful aspect of it all.

Accepting that you need help and that only God can save you is the first step. Similar to what the Psalmist described in the passage above, he was in anguish, his condition worsened, his adversaries despised him, and his sins had overcome him. He then turned to God, realizing that only he could deliver him from his problems. You should do the same, let God work in you, He can change your situation.

Don't allow this price to go in vain. God loves you so much that he paid the most precious for your redemption.

Question:

What is the concept of redemption to you? Choose one option.
1. Redemption means by my deeds and choices I.......................... my life (forfeited, destroyed, lost)
2. Redemption means my life belongs to...................................... (Me, my parents, God)
3. Redemption means God............................. me back because I was lost (brought, bought, borrowed)

Why does God want you to have a second chance?
1. Because he... you (made, created, loves)
2. Because.. needs a second chance (nobody, everybody)

One reason God will redeem you is that he wants you to....................... things right (forget, create, make)

What changes will you make today because of this study?
1...
2...
3...

Personal Notes: Write whatever the Spirit of God lays in your heart, and pray about it

....
....
....
....
....
....
....
....
....
....
....
....
....
....
....
....
....
....
....
....
....
....
....
....
....
....
....
....

Assignment: Memorize. Psalms 25:22
Bravo, you have completed Day 11. Now tick yourself a Pass ▪

Today's Prayer

Lord Teach me to:

Today I am grateful for:

Topic: Feeling Condemned?
Central truth: GOD WILL PARDON YOU.

> *"Jesus entered Jericho and made his way through the town. There was a man there named Zacchaeus. He was the chief tax collector in the region, and he had become very rich. He tried to get a look at Jesus, but he was too short to see over the crowd. So he ran ahead and climbed a sycamore-fig tree beside the road, for Jesus was going to pass that way. When Jesus came by, he looked up at Zacchaeus and called him by name. "Zacchaeus!" he said. "Quick, come down! I must be a guest in your home today." Zacchaeus quickly climbed down and took Jesus to his house in great excitement and joy. But the people were displeased. "He has gone to be the guest of a notorious sinner," they grumbled. Meanwhile, Zacchaeus stood before the Lord and said, "I will give half my wealth to the poor, Lord, and if I have cheated people on their taxes, I will give them back four times as much!" Jesus responded, "Salvation has come to this home today, for this man has shown himself to be a true son of Abraham. For the Son of Man came to seek and save those who are lost." Luke 19:1-10.*

Zacchaeus was a tax collector, a man who collected taxes on behalf of the Roman government. Zacchaeus had a poor reputation among the Israelites because he was a traitor and tax cheat. Tax collectors were unpopular in Jesus' days, because they extorted money from the people and lived an opulent lifestyle envied by all.

Zacchaeus was already guilty in the eyes of the religious authorities and was going to hell. They viewed him as the poster child for sin and someone with whom no one should associate.

But customarily, Jesus ate with Zacchaeus when he went to his home.

How could Jesus hang around swindlers, traitors, and sinners they murmured to themselves? They failed to understand the nature of Jesus' ministry. He came to save the sinner and the lost. Those who are well do not need a doctor, but those who are sick, he said.

You are the very person Jesus came to save if you feel condemned by someone or something that has happened to you. Jesus doesn't condemn you; they condemned him at Calvary in your place. He died on the cross with your sins, imparted to him. He took all your condemnation, judgment, and wrath. (John 8:11)

If you come to the Lord Jesus Christ, confess your sins to him, and turn away from them, you can end any emotions of condemnation you may experience right now, regardless of how your history has been. The blood of Jesus has miraculous healing powers. You don't have to continue in the terrible anguish of condemnation; stop following your emotions and believe what Jesus says.

As he said to Zacchaeus, he says to you, "Today, Salvation has come to your household (doorstep) and it will be the same for you as Simon the Zealot."

Questions:
How does condemnation come? Choose one option.
1. When people believe you have done something......................................
(beautiful, wrong, noble)
2. When you condemn...................................... for what you have done wrong (others, people, yourself)
When people condemn you or you condemn yourself. God doesn't.. you. (kill, punish, condemn).

What is the meaning of Zacchaeus climbing a tree?

1. He was a man of... stature (big, short, low)

2. He wanted to see (..) Jesus (analyze, compare, experience)

3. He wanted to be.................................. by Jesus (condemned, rebuked, seen)

When people condemn you, why do you need to be glad?

1. Because you are the person..wants to visit (Government, Police, Jesus)

2. Because God doesn't..you (embarrass, forsake, condemn)

What changes will you make today because of this study?

1...

2...

3...

Personal Notes: Write whatever the Spirit of God lays in your heart, and pray about it

....

....

....

....

....

....

....

....

....

....

....

....

Assignment: Memorize. Luke 19:10

Bravo, you have completed Day 12. Now tick yourself a Pass

Today's Prayer

Lord Teach me to:

Today I am grateful for:

Topic: Are you depressed?
Central truth: DON'T GIVE UP THERE IS LIGHT AT THE END OF THE TUNNEL.

> *"These things come to mind as I pour out my soul: how I walked with the multitude, leading the procession to the house of God with shouts of joy and praise. Why are you downcast, O my soul? Why the unease within me? Put your hope in God, for I will yet praise Him for the salvation of His presence. O my God, my soul despairs within me. Therefore, I remember You from the land of Jordan and the peaks of Hermon—even from Mount Mizar." Psalms 42:4-6*

> *"Why are you downcast, O my soul? Why the unease within me? Put your hope in God, for I will yet praise Him, my Savior, and my God.: Psalms 42:11*

David wrote the Psalms while fleeing from Absalom, who sought to assassinate him. David was devastated to discover that his son, who had never been his enemy, had turned against him. Because some of his closest friends, including Ahithophel, had sided with Absalom, made it worse.

When people you love take up arms against you, it becomes a battle that is hard to fight. It is difficult to hit back at a loved one who is throwing the kitchen sink and everything at you.

When you are disappointed, betrayed, or vilified by individuals you have always loved and tried to help, despair may set in. However, since depression is an emotional state of mind, you will overcome whatever challenges life hands you.

Being in prison can be hard. You may feel like giving up on life. Your loved ones may disappoint you, and you may have felt betrayed or denigrated by them.

The bad part about depression is that it can affect your mental health and cause social withdrawal, antisocial behavior, and even suicide if it is not treated. Since depression is an emotional state of mind, you will overcome whatever challenges life hands you.

The good news is that you have a wonderful counselor, everlasting father, and prince of peace that will help you if you reach out for his help. (Isaiah 9:6).

David could look up to God and the wonders of his creation to give him hope that if God could make the cape of Mount Hermon, a peak that is always covered in snow and is near Jerusalem, into the beauty and blessing it was to Israel, then God is capable of much more for him.

Questions:

Why is depression a bad emotional feeling? Choose one option.
1. It can lead to.. health issues (physical, mental, social)
2. It can lead to...................................... (isolation, rejection, oppression)
3. It can lead to anti-social.............................. (behaviors, laws, stigmas)

How did David suggest you deal with depression in Psalms 42:11? Choose one option.
1. Put your.......................................in God (problems, anxieties, hope)

When you are depressed, what do you do? Choose one option.
1. Acknowledge that no problem is............................... than God (bigger than, lighter than, more serious)
2. Encourage yourself through the............................... of God (miracles, parables, word).

3. Meditate on 1 Corinthians 10:13, which says:

> *"The temptations in your life are no different from what others experience. And God is faithful. He will not allow the temptation to be more than you can stand. When you are tempted, he will show you a way out so that you can endure."* (NLT)

What changes will you make today because of this study?

1..

2..

3..

Personal Notes: Write whatever the Spirit of God lays in your heart, and pray about it

....
....
....
....
....
....
....
....
....
....
....
....
....
....
....

Assignment: Memorize. 1 Corinthians 10:13

Bravo, you have completed Day 13. Now tick yourself a Pass

Today's Prayer

Lord Teach me to:

Today I am grateful for:

Topic: Are you Fatherless?
Central truth: YOU CAN BECOME A CHILD OF GOD.

> *"But you are our Father, though Abraham does not know us or Israel acknowledge us; you, LORD, are our Father, our Redeemer from of old is your name. Isaiah 63:16 (NIV)*

> *"But to all who believed him and accepted him, he gave the right to become children of God." John 1:12 (NLT)*

Over 70% of children serving time in the US originate from homes where the father is absent or neglectful of his responsibilities as a father. The absence of or inadequate parental supervision of children has been one of the major causes of juvenile delinquency.

Having a father is important for young boys, as it gives them someone to call their father and supports their emotional and intellectual growth.

There are many households where this is a serious issue, and many children are raised by single mothers, who scarcely have the time to take care of them and fulfill the dual duty of mother and father.

If you have ever had a void in your life because of the absence of a father figure, God is expressing his desire to be your father. The Bible says in 1 John 3:1, "See how much our Father loves us, for he names us his children, and such are we." They can't tell that we are God's children, though, because they are from this world.

God loves you and wants to be your father. You will never experience more adoration than this. To help you become the finest person he has created you to be. He wants to lead, guard, encourage, counsel, and occasionally correct you.

Simply inviting God into your life through his son, Jesus Christ, will make you a child of God.

What a blessing!

Questions

Why are fathers important to the lives of children? Choose an option.
1. Fathers provide a sense of.............................. (identity, happiness, enjoyment)
2. Fathers provide, guide, protect, and.. the children. (discipline, punish, tongue lash)
3. Fathers help children develop both educationally and............................ (psychologically, emotionally, and physically)

How do you feel without a father?
1. ....
2...
3...

Why does God want to be your father?
1. Because he............................ you (wants, loves, knows)
2. Because he wants you to be part of his...
(family, congregation, church)

What do you do to make God your father, according to John 1:12?
1. Believe in....................................... (John the Baptist; Jesus Christ; Prophet Elisha)

2. Receive Jesus by asking him into your.................. (heart, business, family)

What changes will you make today because of this study?
1..
2..
3..

Personal Notes: Write whatever the Spirit of God lays in your heart, and pray about it

....
....
....
....
....
....
....
....
....
....
....
....
....
....
....

Assignment: Memorize. 1 John 3:1
Bravo, you have completed Day 14. Now tick yourself a Pass ▇

Today's Prayer

Lord Teach me to:

Today I am grateful for:

Topic: Feeling insecure?
Central truth: YOU CAN FEEL SECURE IN GOD.

> *"Those who live in the shelter of the Most-High will find rest in the shadow of the Almighty. This I declare about the LORD: He alone is my refuge, my place of safety; he is my God, and I trust him. For he will rescue you from every trap and protect you from deadly disease. He will cover you with his feathers. He will shelter you with his wings. His faithful promises are your armor and protection. Do not be afraid of the terrors of the night, nor the arrow that flies in the day. Do not dread the disease that stalks in darkness, nor the disaster that strikes at midday. Though a thousand fall at your side, though ten thousand are dying around you, these evils will not touch you. Just open your eyes and see how the wicked are punished. Psalms 91:1-8.*

Security is one of a man's basic requirements. The assurance that something or someone has got your back. This need is so important that people try to use every known means to achieve a sense of security.

You experience insecurity when you don't feel safe, or when something or someone threatens you. You may feel insecure if you also lack specific possessions that you should have. Most of us experience insecurity occasionally, but many people experience it frequently, according to a Psychology Today article posted online.

He associated this feeling with things like previous childhood experiences, past trauma, recent failures or rejections, loneliness, social anxiety, self-defeating attitudes, perfectionism, and having a partner or parent critical of you. I'll add that having no money or a job can also make people insecure.

You are not alone in your experience, no matter what you are going through. Millions of people have gone through it because they had the support of the appropriate sources.

If you are confident that God has your back, this shows your heart is unwavering. According to the chapter for today, those who remain and find comfort in the Almighty's shelter will remain safe.

David in Psalms 27:1 sums it all up when he said, "The Lord is my light and salvation, who (or what) shall I fear?

Trust in God, and he will keep your heart and mind in perfect peace. Isaiah 26:3.

Questions:
List three things that make you insecure:
1. ....
2..
3..
Why is the feeling of insecurity not unique to you?
1. Everyone has felt................................. sometime or the other (secure, insecure, indifferent)
2. There are always things that will............................ our peace of mind (obscure, threaten, promote)

One way to know someone is insecure is when the person
1. Is unable to trust people
2. Is open to people
3. is unable to trust anyone.

What do you do to achieve peace of mind?

1... in the Lord (Invest, Trust, decide)

2. Talk to him about your.................................. (Dreams, fears, money)

3............................. on God's word. (Concentrate, meditate, expatiate)

What changes will you make today because of this study?

1...

2...

3...

Personal Notes: Write whatever the Spirit of God lays in your heart, and pray about it

....

....

....

....

....

....

....

....

....

....

....

....

....

....

....

....

Assignment: Memorize. Isaiah 26:3.

Bravo, you have completed Day 15. Now tick yourself a Pass ▮

Today's Prayer

Lord Teach me to:

Today I am grateful for:

Topic: Unhappy?
Central truth: GOD WANTS YOU TO BE JOYFUL.

> *"Always be full of joy in the Lord. I say it again—rejoice! Let everyone see that you are considerate in all you do. Remember, the Lord is coming soon. Don't worry about anything; instead, pray about everything. Tell God what you need and thank him for all he has done. Then you will experience God's peace, which exceeds anything we can understand. His peace will guard your hearts and minds as you live in Christ Jesus." And now, dear brothers and sisters, one final thing. Fix your thoughts on what is true, and honorable, and right, and pure, and lovely, and admirable. Think about things that are excellent and worthy of praise. " Philippians 4:4-8 (NLT)*

Several things depress folks. Unpleasant events can cause unhappiness, the death of a loved one, financial ruin, unexplainable losses, and being betrayed by people you love.

For those who have accepted Jesus Christ as their Lord and Savior, He will never change His relationship with them. And that fact is the foundation for joy in every situation - no matter what happens to us or how bad things may seem.

In Paul's letter to the Philippians, he urges Christians to "Rejoice in the Lord always; again, I will say, rejoice!". Philippians 4:4 Even though he wasn't sure what awaited him and was suffering the hardships of prison life, joy filled his letter.

Paul had every reason in the world to be miserable and depressed, but his focus was not on his external conditions, but on his relationship with the Lord. His joy-filled experience didn't match his environment.

If we focus on our difficulties and pain, rather than on Christ, we will become trapped by our circumstances. Amid all the difficulties, Paul had triumphant joy that overcame his circumstances - just as Jesus' triumphant joy over the grave situation did for us in the Sermon on the Mount.

You can find happiness even when incarcerated. Your environment doesn't influence your happiness or misery, but depends on how you choose to live each day. Being anything else would be futile, because you could either live your life mourning your losses, or give God what you still have.

God wants you to be joyful, because, while happiness depends on circumstances, joy is a gift of the spirit that comes from God.

Because you are aware of who you are, you decide to be joyful, despite the circumstances. You know that whatever you are going through right now is only temporary, and that everything will turn out for the best in the end. Romans (8:28)

The devil constantly tells you lies to make you unhappy. He claims you will never be content and that nothing will ever go according to plan for you. All of it is a deception, since God has promised to transform your grief into joy. You can decide whether to believe in God or the devil.

Questions:
What is the difference between happiness and joy?
1. Happiness depends on what happens to you, while joy is
a... of the spirit. (bonus, gift, talent)

2. Happiness is a.. to what happens to you, but Joy is a state of the mind. (result, payment, conclusion).

To either be sad or happy is a.. (choice, reaction, promotion)

What changes will you make today because of this study?
1...
2...
3...

Personal Notes: Write whatever the Spirit of God lays in your heart, and pray about it

....
....
....
....
....
....
....
....
....
....
....
....
....
....
....
....

Assignment: Memorize. Romans 8:28.
Bravo, you have completed Day 16. Now tick yourself a Pass ▪

Today's Prayer

Lord Teach me to:

Today I am grateful for:

Topic: Abandoned?
Central Truth: GOD WILL NEVER ABANDON YOU.

> *"Yet Jerusalem says, "The LORD has deserted us; the Lord has forgotten us." "Never! Can a mother forget her nursing child? Can she feel no love for the child she has borne? But even if that were possible, I would not forget you! See, I have written your name on the palms of my hands. Isaiah 49:14-16 (NLT)*

In a piece for Family Policy Alliance, Stephanie Curry described how her twin sister and she were left at a Los Angeles hospital by their biological mother. Even though she lost her twin sister to rare cancer, she witnessed God's presence throughout it all because of the love and support of her adoptive parents, who educated them about the Lord. God never abandoned her, unlike many abandoned babies who did not survive adulthood. She claims she was "selected" rather than adopted.

According to a preacher, there are no illegitimate children in the eyes of God. God never makes a mistake when he permits a child to be born into the world, even though a mother or father may not desire a child for whatever reason. Children are an inheritance (something you inherit) from God, according to Psalm 127:3-5.

You are therefore unique in God's eyes, regardless of your birth, circumstances, or upbringing. God says that even though you may feel forgotten and abandoned by others and your loved ones, He has written your name on his palms. He not only knows your name, but also sees you every day and adores you for who you are. God is a constant companion who will support you through all your difficulties. He is never a fair-weather friend.

Deuteronomy 4:31 states the Lord is a merciful God who "will not abandon or destroy you or forget the covenant with your ancestors." He powerfully expressed his commitment to his people in this statement. The other promise he made to you was that he would never leave you.

Just trust him and depend on him.

Questions:
Why do people abandon their loved ones? Answer Yes or No

1. Financial pressures?   Yes ▪   No ▪
2. Societal demands?   Yes ▪   No ▪
3. Refusal to take responsibility? Yes ▪ No ▪

Why is being abandoned not the end of life?

1. Because God has a.. for you (blessing, plan, goal)
2. Because you can.................................. whatever you desire to be in life (buy, become, sell)
3. Because your.....................................is not in the hands of men (future, destiny, business)

What does God say he will never do to you?
1. He will.................................... abandon you (always, sometimes, never)
2. He will never...you (kill, forget, dismiss)

What can you say about the way God sees you?
1...
2...

What changes will you make today because of this study?

1..

2..

3..

Personal Notes: Write whatever the Spirit of God lays in your heart, and pray about it

....

....

....

....

....

....

....

....

....

....

....

....

....

....

....

....

Assignment: Memorize. Isaiah 49:15

Bravo, you have completed Day 17. Now tick yourself a Pass ▩

Today's Prayer

_____
_____
_____
_____
_____
_____
_____
_____

Lord Teach me to:

_____
_____
_____
_____
_____
_____
_____
_____
_____

Today I am grateful for:

_____
_____
_____
_____
_____
_____
_____
_____
_____
_____

Topic: Are you afraid?
Central truth: YOU CAN STOP BEING AFRAID.

> *"But now, O Jacob, listen to the LORD who created you. O Israel, the one who formed you says, "Do not be afraid, for I have ransomed you. I have called you by name; you are mine. When you go through deep waters, I will be with you. When you go through rivers of difficulty, you will not drown. When you walk through the fire of oppression, you will not be burned up; the flames will not consume you. For I am the LORD, your God, the Holy One of Israel, your Savior. I gave Egypt as a ransom for your freedom; I gave Ethiopia and Seba in your place. Others were given in exchange for you. I traded their lives for yours because you are precious to me. You are honored, and I love you."*
> *Isaiah 43:1-4 (NLT)*

According to Bible scholars, there are 365 "Fear not" verses in the Bible, one for every day of the year. The devil wants you to feel fear, because if you do, you won't be able to act in faith, and God won't be happy with you (Hebrews 11:6)

Fear of tomorrow is among the most prevalent phobias, paralyzing many people and keeping them from taking chances in life. Fear of heights, the dark, animals, airplanes, and vehicles are some of the more common forms of phobia.

I've never served time in prison, so I don't know how you feel. However, I am aware of what it's like to experience fear and how God has given me the ability to get through my worries. Psalm 34:4 reminds us of God's words. I prayed, and the Lord heard me, and he answered me. He freed me from all my fears. My recommendation to you is to pray and ask God to deliver you from your fears.

Don't be afraid, the Bible commands, no matter what the enemy tries to throw at you. God would not have asked you to do something if it were impossible. You also need to realize that there will be threats to your safety, but rather than being terrified, speak God's word. Hold fast to God's promises, and let the devil know you are entitled to them.

The Bible says resist the devil and he will flee. Do that by the word of God.

Questions:

Why is fear a natural occurrence?
1. There are things that will happen to us that will...us (affect, promote, threaten)
2. Fear is a natural reaction to... (being sure, uncertainty, provocation)
3. The devil wants to destroy your..................................... through fear (affection, worship, faith)

Three things to do when afraid.
1. Remember the... of God (miracles, promises, judgment)
2.. the word of God. (read, confess, sing)
3..................................... upon the word of God. (walk, stand, lie-down)

Why does the Bible have 365 fear not?
1..

What changes will you make today because of this study?
1..
2..
3..

Personal Notes: Write whatever the Spirit of God lays in your heart, and pray about it

....
....
....
....
....
....
....
....
....
....
....
....
....
....
....
....
....
....
....
....
....

Assignment: Memorize. Isaiah 43:2-3
Bravo, you have completed Day 18. Now tick yourself a Pass ■

Today's Prayer

Lord Teach me to:

Today I am grateful for:

Topic: Are you anxious?
Central truth: BE ANXIOUS NO MORE.

> *"Be anxious for nothing but in everything by prayer and supplication, with Thanksgiving, let your request known be made known to God;"* Philippians 4:6
>
> *"So, I tell you, don't worry about everyday life—whether you have enough food, drink, and clothes. Doesn't life consist of more than food and clothing? Look at the birds. They don't need to plant, harvest, or put food in barns, because your heavenly Father feeds them. And you are far more valuable to him than they are. Can all your worries add a single moment to your life? Of course not. Matthew 6: 25-27*

Anxiety is a state of uncertainty backed up by fear. It can lead to serious mental disorders like depression and anxiety disorder. To be anxious is to worry with a sense of apprehension or pessimism that something will work against you or that you cannot achieve certain things.

Anxiety is a condition where negative thoughts and emotions clog your mind. When you are anxious, the problem you are facing doesn't disappear, rather you may end up escalating it. If you are broke and anxious, what the devil brings to your mind is how you're going to lose your house, car, and everything.

After you have done all that is needful and given your best shot, then leave matters in God's unfailing hands. If he provides for the birds, he will provide for you. In Matthew 6, Jesus taught us we shouldn't worry. He wasn't saying that we leave things to chance, but that after we have given our best shot at life, we should trust in God.

The songwriter says, "His eyes are on the sparrow, and I know he watches over you."

Questions:

What is the difference between thinking about a problem and being anxious?
1. When you are anxious, your thoughts are based on fear, but thinking is inevitable
2. Anxiety makes you make wrong decisions

Why is anxiety dangerous to your health?
1. It can lead to anxiety disorder
2. It can lead to depression
3. It can lead to hypertension and heart diseases

What does the Bible say you should do when facing a challenge?
1. Remember God's love for you
2. Remember, you're worth so much to God
3. Remember, he promises to provide for you
4. Remind him about his promises through prayer
5. Thank him in advance for the solution
6. Be joyful

You can talk to a trusted friend or your pastor, who can support you in prayers.

What changes will you make today because of this study?

1..
2..
3..

Personal Notes: Write whatever the Spirit of God lays in your heart, and pray about it

....
....
....
....
....
....
....
....
....
....
....
....
....
....
....
....
....
....
....
....
....
....
....

Assignment: Memorize. Philippians 4:6.
Bravo, you have completed Day 19. Now tick yourself a Pass ▮

Today's Prayer

Lord Teach me to:

Today I am grateful for:

Topic: Feeling Lost?
Central Truth: JESUS CAME TO SEEK AND SAVE THE LOST.

"To illustrate the point further, Jesus told them this story: "A man had two sons. The younger son told his father, 'I want my share of your estate now before you die.' So, his father agreed to divide his wealth between his sons. "A few days later this younger son packed all his belongings and moved to a distant land, and there he wasted all his money in wild living. About the time his money ran out, a great famine swept over the land, and he began to starve. He persuaded a local farmer to hire him, and the man sent him into his fields to feed the pigs. The young man became so hungry that even the pods he was feeding the pigs looked good to him. But no one gave him anything. "When he finally came to his senses, he said to himself, 'At home, even the hired servants have food enough to spare, and here I am dying of hunger! I will go home to my father and say, "Father, I have sinned against both heaven and you, and I am no longer worthy of being called your son. Please take me on as a hired servant."' "So, he returned home to his father. And while he was still a long way off, his father saw him coming. Filled with love and compassion, he ran to his son, embraced him, and kissed him. His son said to him, 'Father, I have sinned against both heaven and you, and I am no longer worthy of being called your son. "But his father said to the servants, 'Quick! Bring the finest robe in the house and put it on him. Get a ring for his finger and sandals for his feet. And kill the calf we have been fattening. We must celebrate with a feast, for this son of mine was dead and has now returned to life. He was lost, but now he is found.' So, the party began. Luke 15:11-24

Losing your bearing or direction is what it means to be lost. Before GPS, you had to ask for directions whenever you got lost. You might never arrive at your destination if you choose not to ask for help. That is the way life is.

We all need direction, especially concerning issues that will affect our destiny.

You are privileged because it was because of people like you that Jesus came. So when you're feeling lost and don't know where else to turn, remember that. Many people face the issue of believing they are in control of their actions and destinations. The Bible warns that there is a path that appears suitable for men, but leads to destruction.

Jesus came to Earth to save the lost and bring them home to the Lord. Jesus is the same as he was, and will still find us when we're lost. Find comfort knowing that whenever you feel down, you have a personal Savior, which should make you feel a lot better.

There will be times when you feel lost, baffled, and empty. However, remember that you must rely on God's word to help you get through these times. If you need a reminder, mark this verse in your Bible. Luke 19:10.

Waste no more time; "Arise and come back to God." God has always stretched out his hands to welcome you.

Questions:
Name three things the prodigal son did wrong. Choose one option.

1. He didn't.. for his time (apply, wait, run)
2. He took his inheritance and.. to a far country away (traveled, relocated, absconded)
3. He didn't want his father to... his life anymore (bless, control, manipulate)

What did the prodigal son do that was right? Choose one option.

1. He came to his.. senses
(true, real, right)

2. He decided to... to his father's house
(return, write, send a message)

3. He.. himself and was ready to
become a servant (humbled, satisfied, controlled)

4. He apologized and asked for..
(forgiveness, restoration, more money)

What changes will you make today because of this study?

1...

2...

3...

Personal Notes: Write whatever the Spirit of God lays in your heart, and pray about it

....

....

....

....

....

....

....

....

....

....

....

....

....

....

....

Assignment: Memorize. Luke 19:10.

Bravo, you have completed Day 20. Now tick yourself a Pass

Today's Prayer

Lord Teach me to:

Today I am grateful for:

Topic: Are you angry?
Central truth: JESUS CAN GIVE YOU PEACE.

> *There was no water for the people to drink at that place, so they rebelled against Moses and Aaron. The people blamed Moses and said, we wish we had died in the Lord's presence with our brothers! Did you bring the Lord's people into this wilderness to die, along with all our livestock? Why did you make us leave Egypt and bring us here to this terrible place? This land has no grain, figs, grapes, or pomegranates. And there is no water to drink! Moses and Aaron turned away from the people and went to the entrance of the Tabernacle, where they fell face down on the ground. Then the glorious presence of the Lord appeared to them, and the Lord said to Moses, you and Aaron must take the staff and assemble the entire community. As the people watch, command the rock over there to pour out its water. You will get enough water from the rock to satisfy all the people and their livestock. So Moses did as he was told. He took the staff from the place where it was kept before the Lord. Then he and Aaron summoned the people to come and gather at the rock. Listen, you rebels he shouted! Must we bring you water from this rock? Then Moses raised his hand and struck the rock twice with the staff, and water gushed out. So, all the people and their livestock drank their fill. "But the Lord said to Moses and Aaron because you did not trust me enough to demonstrate my holiness to the people of Israel, you will not lead them into the land I am giving them! Numbers 20:2-12.*

Both pleasant and negative feelings can arise from being angry. When you experience positive rage, your lack of progress irritates you or by the unjust treatment of others. Negative rage is incredibly harmful.

The Israelites complained to Moses in the wilderness in today's chapter. These were a group of people whom God had kindly freed from servitude via heroic deeds and carried them across the Red Sea.

They had seen for themselves the might of God, but all they could do was complain about what He hadn't yet done. Like that, you undoubtedly know some folks.

God gave Moses the commandment to speak to the rock to bring water, but out of resentment towards the people, Moses hit the rock twice. Since he disregarded God's commands, he was punished and warned he wouldn't be permitted to enter the promised land. Although the frequent murmuring of the people irritated Moses, God would not pardon him for acting in anger. Even though other people and your environment could annoy you, what matters is what comes next. It is not sinful to be furious.

Everyone struggles with anger. Instead of reacting with harsh words and deeds that leave us feeling guilty and ashamed, we might pause and turn to Scripture for guidance. The Bible contains a wealth of instructions about controlling emotions, including wrath. James 1:19 and Ephesians 4:31 are only a few.

Jesus wants you to live in peace, no matter what things they have done to you. "My peace I give to you; my peace, I leave with you," he declares.

Remember, it is uncontrollable anger that is responsible for most crime and violence, but Jesus specializes in turning people around.

Questions
What made Moses angry? Choose one option
1. The people were constantly............................. (Fighting, Murmuring, Laughing)

2. The people were.................................. in their demands (Obstinate, Considerate, Confused)

3. Nothing.. them. (Satisfied, Fooled, Complimented)

Why did God not hold the people responsible for Moses' anger?
Choose one option

1. Moses had a .... (Choice, Voice, Assistant)
2. God doesn't accept.. (Complaints, Show- off, Buck-passing).
3. You are.. for your actions (Excused, Responsible, Ignored)

When we act in anger, we

1. Are likely to do something we will regret
2. Are likely to offend God
3. Are likely to do something destructive

What changes will you make today because of this study?

1...
2...
3...

Personal Notes: Write whatever the Spirit of God lays in your heart, and pray about it

....
....
....
....
....
....
....
....

Assignment: Memorize. Ephesians 4:26

Bravo, you have completed Day 21. Now tick yourself a Pass ▮

Today's Prayer

Lord Teach me to:

Today I am grateful for:

Topic: Have you been abused?
Central truth: JESUS CAN GIVE YOU A FRESH START.

> *"He that is in Christ Jesus is a new creation, old things are passed away, behold, all things have become new." 2 Corinthians 5:17*
>
> *"But forget all that—it is nothing compared to what I am going to do. For I am about to do a brand-new thing. See, I have already begun! Do you not see it? I will make a pathway through the wilderness for my people to come home. I will create rivers for them in the desert!" Isaiah 43:18-19*

According to reports, one out of every seven kids encounters some kind of abuse or neglect. In 2020, 3.6 million cases of child abuse were reported, but 1,750 children died because of abuse and neglect.

Abuse incidents have been occurring for some time, but the frequency and scope are entirely new. Family dysfunction and poor parenting are the major causes of many abuse instances.

If you have experienced abuse, I can relate to the suffering you have gone through, especially since mental violence is more severe than physical abuse. Being an abuse victim has its drawbacks, one of which is that you frequently blame yourself for what you went through.

But thousands of victims of abuse have recovered well. Forgiving yourself and others who have wounded you should come first. Second, you do not depend on your background. Like Oprah Winfrey and countless others, you can shine despite your history.

When you put your faith in Christ, you become a new person. The new person, who is now on the scene and ready to shine for God's glory, has replaced the old person harmed by misuse and abused, and has been buried with Christ in his death.

No matter how messed up you may feel, you are the person Jesus seeks to turn your ashes into beauty and sorrow to joy.

Questions

Why is abuse rampant these days? Choose one option.
1... families (Quarreling, divorced, dysfunctional)
2. Failed.. (marriages, society, parenting)

What does the Bible say will happen to you? Choose one option.

1. Old things will be................................. (passed away, ignored, thrown away)
2... will become new (Your face, Relationships, All things)
3. You can start................................. in Christ Jesus (Afresh, Rejoicing, Dancing)

To overcome abuse, what do you do?

1... those who hurt you (Prosecute, Condemn, Forgive)
2. Forgive yourself and stop feeling...................... (Shy, Annoyed, Guilty)
3. Ask Jesus to clean your heart of the................... (Hurt, Hatred, Envy)

What changes will you make today because of this study?

1...
2...
3...
Personal Notes: Write whatever the Spirit of God lays in your heart, and pray about it

....
....
....
....
....
....
....

....
....
....
....
....
....
....
....
....
....
....
....
....
....
....
....
....
....
....
....
....
....
....
....
....
....
....

Assignment: Memorize. 2 Corinthians 5:17
Bravo, you have completed Day 22. Now tick yourself a Pass

Today's Prayer

Lord Teach me to:

Today I am grateful for:

Topic: Are you Hurting?

Central truth: HE WILL COMFORT YOU WHEN YOU ARE HURTING.

> *"Hannah, why are you crying?" her husband Elkanah asked. "Why won't you eat? Why is your heart so grieved? Am I not better to you than ten sons?" So, after they had finished eating and drinking in Shiloh, Hannah stood up. Now Eli the priest was sitting on a chair by the doorpost of the temple of the LORD. In her bitter distress, Hannah prayed to the LORD and wept with many tears. And she made a vow, pleading, "O LORD of Hosts, if only You will look upon the affliction of Your maidservant and remember me, not forgetting Your maidservant but giving her a son, then I will dedicate him to the LORD all the days of his life, and no razor shall ever come over his head."*
>
> *As Hannah kept praying before the LORD, Eli watched her mouth. Hannah was praying in her heart, and though her lips were moving, her voice could not be heard. So, Eli thought she was drunk and said to her, "How long will you be drunk? Put away your wine!" "No, my lord," Hannah replied. "I am a woman oppressed in spirit. I have not had any wine or strong drink, but I have poured out my soul before the LORD.*
>
> *Do not take your servant for a wicked woman. For all this time, I have been praying out of the depth of my anguish and grief." "Go in peace," Eli replied, "and may the God of Israel grant the petition you have asked of Him."*
>
> *"May your maidservant find favor with you," said Hannah. Then she went on her way, and began eating again, and her face was no longer downcast. 1 Samuel 1:8-17.*

Hannah's tale is an example of the grief and pains people experience through no fault of their own. God had closed Hannah's womb to prevent her from producing offspring like Peninnah, her mate. They made fun of her and teased her for being "barren," which caused her to cry until she couldn't cry anymore.

Hannah describes how she cried out to God "out of the depth of anguish and grief" because she could not bear the thought of being childless. Children were important in Jewish culture, as they helped their mothers survive in an agrarian environment. It was a sign of helplessness if a woman did not have children.

Hannah was not religious in her prayers. She told God exactly how she felt, and bantered with God, vowing that if God gave her a son, she would give him to God for the rest of his life.

Perhaps because you are imprisoned, your family and friends turn their backs on you. I cannot even imagine how badly that will hurt you. You can find solace despite how miserable you are feeling. Jesus Christ is ready to console you; God hasn't abandoned you just because your loved ones have. Allow Jesus to show his love for you. Because your heavenly father loves you more than anyone else, find acceptance and love in Christ. He vowed to be with you in your suffering and comfort us. (2 Corinthians 1:3).

The Holy Spirit can comfort you, and He brings healing and serenity to your wounded heart. The Comforter has been with us ever since Jesus died on the cross to atone for our sins. You can find unfathomable and wonderful comfort by resting in the power of the Holy Spirit.

Hannah knew that turning to God was the only way to find solace from her misery and agony. She had seven children besides "Samuel," one of history's greatest prophets. God turned her pain into joy, and He made her suffering joyful.

You too can experience the same thing, because God never changes!

Questions:

When Hannah was hurt, what did she do?

1. She went to the.., the place of prayer (Court, Shiloh, Jerusalem)
2. She didn't... Peninnah back (Report, Ridicule, Fight)

Why was it impossible for her husband, Elkanah, to help her case?

1. Only God can turn her story into........................ (Mockery, Glory, Payback)
2. The............................. to her problem was in the hand of God and not man. (Solution, Promises, Resources)

Why were Hannah's prayers unique?
1. She poured out her............................... to God (Story, Heart, Tears)
2. She made a.................................... with God (Promise, Vow, Complaint)

In your own words, why do you think God allowed Hannah to go through all that pain?

1..
2..

What changes will you make today because of this study?
1..
2..
3..

Personal Notes: Write whatever the Spirit of God lays in your heart, and pray about it

....
....
....
....
....
....
....
....
....
....
....
....
....

Assignment: Memorize. 1 Samuel 1:10-11
Bravo, you have completed Day 23. Now tick yourself a Pass

Today's Prayer

Lord Teach me to:

Today I am grateful for:

Topic: Do you feel guilty?
Central truth: JESUS CAME TO WIPE AWAY YOUR GUILT!

> *"And the LORD said to Moses, "If someone sins and acts unfaithfully against the LORD by deceiving his neighbor regarding a deposit or security entrusted to him or stolen, or if he extorts his neighbor or finds lost property and lies about it and swears falsely, or if he commits any such sin that a man might commit— once he has sinned and becomes guilty, he must return what he has stolen or taken by extortion, or the deposit entrusted to him, or the lost property he found, or anything else about which he has sworn falsely.*
>
> *He must make restitution in full, add a fifth of the value, and pay it to the owner on the day he acknowledges his guilt. Then he must bring to the priest his guilt offering to the LORD: an unblemished ram of proper value from the flock. In this way, the priest will make atonement for him before the LORD, and he will be forgiven for anything he may have done to incur guilt." Leviticus 6:1-7*

Once you break God's law, you are guilty in the eyes of God, whether you are aware or ignorant. Guilt is one of the strongest negative emotions one can ever experience. This is important because nobody is perfect, and we all make mistakes but what is crucial is that we are accountable for our actions.

Because of this, God commanded his people in the Old Testament to prepare a guilt sacrifice that should make up for or atone for their mistakes, whether intentional or unintentional. Unfortunately, such a sacrifice had to be repeated frequently to clear one's conscience of guilt.

If you have a conscience, you will feel bad for doing things you know you shouldn't have done. A guilty conscience is harmful. As a result, God sent Jesus to the Cross of Calvary to make an atoning sacrifice for our sins and other transgressions.

So, you don't need to carry that load of guilt anymore. If you acknowledge you made a mistake, there is provision for your atonement and the writer of Hebrews says:

> *"Let us go right into the presence of God with sincere hearts fully trusting him. For our guilty consciences have been sprinkled with Christ's blood to make us clean, and our bodies have been washed with pure water." Hebrews 10:22*

Once you come to Christ Jesus and acknowledge your misdeeds, his blood washes you from a guilty conscience, and your heart is cleansed. You can live with a pure conscience, knowing God has pardoned your sins and set you free.

This is the essence of being forgiven!

Questions:

Why is guilt very important?

1. Everyone makes.. (Mistakes, Promises, Plans)
2. Our.............................. judges us when we do what isn't right. (Heart, Mind, Conscience)
3. Guilt is a................................ load to carry (Light, Uncommon, Heavy)

Why is ignorance not an excuse for being guilty?

1. God in his holiness must............................ with sin. (Ignore, Deal with, Punish)
2. Every misdeed is................................. God's Law (Fulfilling, Breaking, Complimenting)

What did Jesus do to free you from a guilty conscience?

1. He....................... the price for your offense (Paid, Mortgaged, Sold)
2. He washed your heart and conscience with his.................................... (Water, Blood, Soap)

What changes will you make today because of this study?

1..

2..

3..

Personal Notes: Write whatever the Spirit of God lays in your heart, and pray about it

....

....

....

....

....

....

....

....

....

....

....

....

....

....

....

....

....

....

....

....

Assignment: Memorize. Hebrews 10:22

Bravo, you have completed Day 24. Now tick yourself a Pass ■

Today's Prayer

_____
_____
_____
_____
_____
_____
_____
_____

Lord Teach me to:

_____
_____
_____
_____
_____
_____
_____
_____
_____

Today I am grateful for:

_____
_____
_____
_____
_____
_____
_____
_____
_____

Topic: Are you Lonely?
Central truth: JESUS WANTS TO BE WITH YOU.

> *"Then the LORD said to Moses, "Come up to Me on the mountain and stay here, so that I may give you the tablets of stone, with the law and commandments I have written for their instruction."*
> *Exodus 24:12*
>
> *"Even if my father and mother abandon me, the LORD will hold me close." Psalms 27:10*

Prisoners kept in isolation cells for extended periods may become broken. Losing touch with others can be a punishment sometimes more severe than physical punishment, since God wired us for relationships and communities.

I once watched a video of elderly people in a Western country ordering coffee, pizza, or cakes, not because they need them, but because the delivery person may spend some time chatting with them, since they are alone. However, being alone in a crowd is the worst form of loneliness. You are among people, but you know you don't belong and that there is no love lost between you and the members of your group. This kind of loneliness can lead to depression and untimely death.

Both good and bad loneliness exist. Positive loneliness is when you set aside time to be with God and avoid other people and distractions. There are some spiritual encounters that you can only have by yourself with God. God requested Moses come by himself when it was time for him to receive the commandments. John "the Beloved" had to be sent to the Island of Patmos alone when the Book of Revelation was to be revealed.

Therefore, if you're feeling lonely, consider whether God is using the situation to draw your attention. God may have needed your attention, but you were too preoccupied conversing with others. In contrast, if you are feeling lonely because your friends and family have abandoned you, realize that God wants to fill the void their departure has created.

Jesus Christ can be the source of your strength when you are lonely. The father wants you to have an intimate relationship with his Son and enrich your friendship with others. God created you unto himself, he wants to walk with you and live on the inside with you.

A close relationship with Jesus Christ is the only thing that has the power to satisfy the human heart. Given how much he loves us, God does not want any of his children to feel lonely. He will provide you with godly relationships and provide an anchor for your soul through the word of God, so you don't have to turn to drugs, alcohol, or suicide.

Lord, I'm lonely and need you right now. You promise never to leave or abandon me. You said I have everything while I have you. All I want is for you to embrace me in your arms, O dear God.

Question:

In your own words, what do you understand by loneliness? Choose one option

1. When you are.......................... with no one to talk to (rich, famous, alone)
2. When you are amongst people but... from them (Far, Disconnected, Barred)

When someone is abandoned and alone what can happen? Choose one option

1. it can lead to.. (Oppression, Hallucination, Depression)
2. It can lead to early... (Retirement, Death, Frustration)

In what situation can loneliness be positive? Choose one option
1. When God seeks your... (Money, family, Attention)
2. When you are too..................................... with other things but God (Busy, Close, Playful)

When people desert you, what does God do?

1. He wants to.. the vacuum left by them (Cancel, Occupy, Make-Up)

2. He wants to.. to you privately and not in a crowd (Run, Speak, Shout)

What changes will you make today because of this study?

1..

2..

3..

Personal Notes: Write whatever the Spirit of God lays in your heart, and pray about it

....
....
....
....
....
....
....
....
....
....
....
....
....
....
....
....
....
....
....
....

Assignment: Memorize. Psalms 27:10

Bravo, you have completed Day 25. Now tick yourself a Pass

Today's Prayer

Lord Teach me to:

Today I am grateful for:

Topic: Feeling Hopeless?
Central truth: LET JESUS BE YOUR HOPE.

> *"As the deer pants for streams of water, so my soul longs after You, O God. My soul thirsts for God, the living God. When shall I come and appear in God's presence? My tears have been my food both day and night, while men ask me all day long, "Where is your God?" These things come to mind as I pour out my soul: how I walked with the multitude, leading the procession to the house of God with shouts of joy and praise. Why are you downcast, O my soul? Why the unease within me? Put your hope in God, for I will yet praise Him for the salvation of His presence. Psalms 42:1-5*

> *"Vindicate me, O God, and plead my case against an ungodly nation, deliver me from deceitful and unjust men. For You are the God of my refuge. Why have You rejected me? Why must I walk in sorrow because of the enemy's oppression? Send out Your light and Your truth; let them lead me. Let them bring me to Your holy mountain, and to the place where You dwell. Then I will go to the altar of God, to God, my greatest joy. I will praise You with the harp, O God, my God. Why are you downcast, O my soul? Why the unease within me? Put your hope in God, for I will yet praise Him, my Savior and my God. Psalms 43:1-5*

Some states that a man can lose everything and still recover, but when you take away his hope, all is lost. People who commit suicide do so because they are in a dismal situation and cannot see any relief from their circumstances.

One can understand David's emotions when he wrote these two Psalms by reading them. His hope was all but gone, because he had experienced oppression, betrayal, and injustice. He was depressed and in tears because the people he trusted had betrayed him. But he did the one thing by turning to God, which changed his sense of helplessness. Like a deer thirsting for water, he yearned for God.

What do you do when everything you believed in seemed vanished, and all hope seems lost?

God uses the experiences of our lives to develop us. This includes the periods of trial, our time in the dark room, so to speak. When nothing seems clear, look toward God instead of trying to solve it yourself. We know that God will have done marvelous work in us.

No matter our color, language, country, state, or social standing, as humans, we all have to deal with hardships in life. We must realize, though, that only God takes care of us; He gives us life and delivers us from the sorrows that weigh us down. God controls and directs history. He urges us to focus solely on Him, since it is only in Him that we can find a future and hope.

When times are hard, hope keeps us from giving up. We can't survive without hope. After all, hope keeps us going. Hope gets us up in the morning. It is what enables us to get up and show up.

David spoke to himself and said to his soul, "Why are you downcast?" It is important to talk to yourself sometimes because your soul has an "ear".

Encourage yourself by reading the Bible, and remember that nothing in life is permanent. This too will pass away.

Meditate on Psalms 42 and 43 and draw strength from them.

Questions:

What does it mean to be hopeless? Choose one option

1. When all you put your.. upon disappoints you (Money, Trust, Stake)
2. When there is no... at the end of the tunnel (Light, Sun, Moon)

Why is hopelessness such a serious situation? Choose one option
1. It can lead to.. (Hypertension, Brain Damage, Suicide)

When hopelessness sets in, what do you do? Choose one option.

1..................................... the word of God to your soul (Write, Speak, Confirm)
2. Turn to... in prayers (A friend, A Pastor, God)
3. Meditate on Psalms............................. and...

What changes will you make today because of this study?

1...
2...
3...

Personal Notes: Write whatever the Spirit of God lays in your heart, and pray about it

....
....
....
....
....
....
....
....
....
....
....
....
....
....
....
....
....
....
....

Assignment: Memorize. Psalms 43:5
Bravo, you have completed Day 26. Now tick yourself a Pass

Today's Prayer

Lord Teach me to:

Today I am grateful for:

Topic: Feeling Forgotten?
Central truth: YOU ARE NOT FORGOTTEN.

The next morning, the dreams disturbed Pharaoh. So, he called for all the magicians and wise men of Egypt. When Pharaoh told them his dreams, not one of them could tell him what they meant.

Finally, the king's chief cupbearer spoke up. "Today I have been reminded of my failure," he told Pharaoh. "Sometime ago, you were angry with the chief baker and me, and you imprisoned us in the palace of the captain of the guard. One night, the chief baker and I each had a dream, and each dream had its own meaning. There was a young Hebrew man with us in the prison who was a slave of the captain of the guard. We told him our dreams, and he told us what each of our dreams meant. And everything happened just as he had predicted. I was restored to my position as cupbearer, and the chief baker was executed and impaled on a pole."

Pharaoh sent for Joseph at once, and he was quickly brought from the prison. After he shaved and changed his clothes, he went in and stood before Pharaoh. Then Pharaoh said to Joseph, "I had a dream last night, and no one here can tell me what it means. But I have heard that when you hear about a dream, you can interpret it."
Genesis 41:8-15

I advise reading the entirety of Genesis chapters 40 and 41 to completely grasp this tale. The cupbearer was a devoted servant of Pharaoh, and Joseph had helped him while he was imprisoned and asked that he be remembered. However, the cupbearer completely forgot about Joseph for two whole years when God sent Pharaoh a dream that no one else in his realm could understand but Joseph.

If we rely on other people, we can end up being forgotten, not because those other people are bad, but because they should look out for no. 1 because that is the Golden Rule. The tendency of people to take up your matter pales compared to their difficulties in our individualistic, rat-race society.

Don't blame others for forgetting about you when you are in need. Unless people have found solutions to their problems, they care less about what others are going through. According to the Bible, the person who puts their trust in men, gains strength from mere flesh, and has a heart that turns away from the LORD is cursed. Jeremiah 17.

Do not be concerned if others forget you, since God has got your back. Don't harbor resentment toward them, and instead turn to God, the source of your strength, rather than man. When it was time, God caused Pharaoh to dream, which elevated Joseph to fame.

If you feel forgotten by God, doubt and disobedience come closer. It becomes tempting to dull the pain with drugs, alcohol, food, and unconstructive behavior. You might even consider suicide a way out. I plead with you not to go down that road. That is never what God would want. In your pain, in your feeling of hopelessness, understand that God still wants to use you. He has you alive for a purpose. No matter how dark the jail or long the prison sentence is, God has not forgotten you. He still wants to use you.

No matter how dark your situation is, you do not know what God has in store. All I can assure you of is that he has not forgotten. Keep representing him. Keep serving. Your way out of the dungeon is linked to that. If you bury yourself in pity, anger, or isolation, you will miss what God wants to do.

This season, God will think about you. You only need to ask in prayer!

Questions:
Why do people forget about us? Choose one option

1. They have their own.. (Challenges, Cross, Children)
2. There is a natural tendency to look out for...................... and not others (Family, Friends, Ourselves)

When people forget about you, what will God do? Choose one option

1. He will cause you to be..
(Celebrated, Remembered, Nominated)
2. He will make someone have a... only you can
solve (Car, House, {Problem)

In your own words, what does Jeremiah 17:5 mean to you?
1..
2..

What changes will you make today because of this study?
1..
2..
3..

Personal Notes: Write whatever the Spirit of God lays in your heart, and pray about it

....
....
....
....
....
....
....
....
....
....
....
....
....
....
....
....
....
....
....

Assignment: Memorize. Nehemiah 13:22
Bravo, you have completed Day 27. Now tick yourself a Pass ■

Today's Prayer

_____
_____
_____
_____
_____
_____
_____
_____

Lord Teach me to:

_____
_____
_____
_____
_____
_____
_____
_____
_____
_____

Today I am grateful for:

_____
_____
_____
_____
_____
_____
_____
_____
_____
_____

Topic: Discouraged?
Central Truth: JESUS WILL ENCOURAGE YOU.

> *"Three days later, when David and his men arrived home at their town of Ziklag, they found that the Amalekites had made a raid into the Negev and Ziklag; they had crushed Ziklag and burned it to the ground. They had carried off the women and children and everyone else but without killing anyone. When David and his men saw the ruins and realized what had happened to their families, they wept until they could weep no more. David's two wives, Ahinoam from Jezreel and Abigail, the widow of Nabal from Carmel, were among those captured. David was now in great danger because all his men were very bitter about losing their sons and daughters, and they began to talk of stoning him. But David found strength in the Lord his God.*
> *1 Samuel 30:1-6. (NLT)*

In today's passage, we see David in a dire situation where all his men considered killing him because they blamed him for their predicament. They forgot quickly that it was David that had molded them into a formidable force. They forgot it was not David that invited the Amalekites to raid their camp and take away all their wives and children. Anyway, as a leader, the buck stopped with David, who also lost his wives and children to the raiding band.

When faced with discouragement, David had to decide whether to give in to despair or stand up and take on the task at hand. We are told that he strengthened his faith in God.

In a time of need, instead of blaming others, he went to God. If you read the complete chapter, you'll learn that he saved the entire family and brought back many spoils of war.

There will always be events that put our peace in jeopardy and dishearten us. We cannot predetermine certain actions, because we have no control over them. Therefore, when things do not go according to our plans, we get frustrated.

You can choose to give up and submit, or you can resist and press on. You'll never know if something is possible unless you try. To stay still is to concede defeat, but when you try, you could first fail, but as you persevere, you will succeed.

According to legend, Thomas Edison, a famous inventor, attempted the electric bulb experiment 1000 times before he was successful. When asked why he didn't give up, he replied that every failure taught him a new strategy that wouldn't work.

This is the attitude God wants you to adopt. Because God is on your side, never give up.

God does not want us stuck in anger or any other negative feelings we may have. We should go before God as we are, not pretending to be someone we are not. If we are honest with God in prayer, we will feel deep freedom and a deeper relationship with God.

Questions:

What are the things that tend to discourage us?

1. When things do not go according to............................ (Progress, Plan, Imagination)
2. When you are caught...................................by an unforeseen disaster. (Pants down, Off Guard, Exposed)
3. When all we have been.. suddenly disappears (Working for, Acquiring, Possessing)

When we are discouraged, what must we not do?
1.. others for our misfortune (Hate, Blame, Condemn)
2. Pass the..to others (Losses, Buck, Cross)
3. Do not act in.. (Denial. Unbelief, Shock)

When we are discouraged, what must we do?

1.. what has happened and turn to God (Accept, Condemn, Appraise)

2.. yourself with the word of God (Discourage, Encourage, Cover)

Why is discouragement something to be fought?

1. No condition in life is.. (Predictable, Permanent, Permissible)

2. Discouragement can be a steppingstone to.. (Victory, Recovery, Glory)

What changes will you make today because of this study?

1..

2..

3..

Personal Notes: Write whatever the Spirit of God lays in your heart, and pray about it

....
....
....
....
....
....
....
....
....
....
....
....
....
....
....
....

Assignment: Memorize. 1 Samuel 30:6 (KJV)

Bravo, you have completed Day 28. Now tick yourself a Pass ▣

Today's Prayer

Lord Teach me to:

Today I am grateful for:

Topic: Ashamed?
Central truth: JESUS BORE YOUR SHAME.

> *"The Sovereign LORD has spoken to me, and I have listened. I have not rebelled or turned away. I offered my back to those who beat me and my cheeks to those who pulled out my beard. I did not hide my face from mockery and spitting. Because the Sovereign LORD helps me, I will not be disgraced. Therefore, I have set my face like a stone, determined to do his will. And I know that I will not be put to shame. He who gives me justice is near. Who will dare to bring charges against me now? Where are my accusers? Let them appear! See, the Sovereign LORD is on my side! Who will declare me guilty? All my enemies will be destroyed, like old clothes eaten by moths!*
> *Isaiah 50:5-9 (NLT)*

According to the dictionary, shame is an unpleasant sense of humiliation or grief caused by an awareness of improper or unwise behavior. Shame is the opposite of pride and respect, because it lowers our self-esteem.

According to Genesis 3, one effect of the fall of man was that he realized his nakedness. He attempted to hide his shame by sewing together fig leaves, but this was ineffective. God had to sacrifice an animal and cover man's disgrace with its skin.

One of the enemy's attacks against you is to make sure you are put to shame. He wants your marriage to fail; he wants your finances to crumble; he wants your health to be unstable, and everything about you should be shrouded in shame.

The devil wants you to be ashamed of every mistake or poor choice you have ever made, or that those you care about (especially family) have made. He wants you to feel humiliated because you were raised in a dysfunctional household or have a specific family background, and that you have committed some heinous crimes that you should not be proud of.

The good news is that Jesus took our shame upon himself, as the scripture taught us in today's reading. You will comprehend the humiliation he had to go through solely because of you, if you see the movie "The Passion of the Christ."

If you receive a speeding ticket fine and someone pays it, it releases you from your obligation to pay the fine. Jesus did the same thing when he died on the cross at Calvary, taking your shame upon himself so that you could live in glory and honor.

Because he took it away. Stop wearing the badge of shame. Just smile and keep your head up!

Questions:

Why does the enemy want you to be ashamed?

1. Shame doesn't allow you to.................... your full potential (Climb, Reach, Collect)
2. Shame makes you to.. from God (Run, Hide, Disappear)

Why do you not need to be ashamed anymore?

1. Because you are not above making.. (Passes, Mistakes, Trouble)
2. Jesus has...................................... your shame (canceled, postponed, suspended)
3. The fine for your shame has been..................... in full (Covered, Paid, Hidden)

Why is shame such a negative emotion?

1. Shame results in.. (Guilt, Pride, Frustration)
2. Shame makes you think............................ about yourself (More, Less, High)

What do you do when you remember your past mistakes or that of your parents?

1. Remember that Jesus has paid the.................................... in full (Money, Price, Fine)
2. Plead the blood of Jesus.

What changes will you make today because of this study?

1...
2...
3...

Personal Notes: Write whatever the Spirit of God lays in your heart, and pray about it

....
....
....
....
....
....
....
....
....
....
....
....
....
....
....
....

Assignment: Memorize. John 19:30
Bravo, you have completed Day 29. Now tick yourself a Pass

Today's Prayer

Lord Teach me to:

Today I am grateful for:

Topic: Weary?
Central Truth: GOD WILL RENEW YOUR STRENGTH AND GIVE YOU REST.

> *"To whom will you compare me? Who is my equal?" asks the Holy One. Look up into the heavens. Who created all the stars? He brings them out like an army, one after another, calling each by its name. Because of his great power and incomparable strength, not a single one is missing. O Jacob, how can you say the LORD does not see your troubles? O Israel, how can you say God ignores your rights? Have you never heard? Have you never understood? The LORD is the everlasting God, the Creator of all the earth. He never grows weak or weary. No one can measure the depths of his understanding. He gives power to the weak and strength to the powerless. Even youths will become weak and tired, and young men will fall in exhaustion. But those who trust in the LORD will find new strength. They will soar high on wings like eagles. They will run and not grow weary. They will walk and not faint. Isaiah 40:25-31*

When you watch a boxing match, a boxer's stamina and ability to stay in the ring for an extended period can help him win. This is because, regardless of how great the boxer may appear, if he lacks stamina, he will quickly wear out and be knocked out by a less skilled but more durable opponent.

Life is a marathon, not a 100-meter dash, and only those with the endurance to stick it out will prevail in the end. We need to regularly renew our strength, because our energy levels weaken. Many things drain our energy, including obligations, responsibilities, tragedies, and social pressures, but we must persevere.

Unfortunately, many people turn to alcohol, drugs, or other substances to regain their strength. However, the Bible promises that "those who wait on God shall renew their strength."

To wait on God, one must first recognize who he is and what he is capable of. The only person who can assist you is He, the Creator and Sovereign LORD. Second, you admit you are powerless to help yourself and in need of His help. Third, ask God in prayer to give you new strength. Finally, you want to express your gratitude to God in advance for providing you with the strength to fight life's battles.

It's not a problem if you're tired. The issue is when you stay that way and give up. And that's not what you want, is it?

Questions:

Why is it that we get tired in life?

1. There are life's responsibilities and.................................... (Promises, Battles, Events)
2. Our strength cannot............................ forever (run, be ignited, last)

What do you do when you are tired in life?
1.. you can't help yourself (Anticipate, Acknowledge, Assume)
2. Acknowledge that only........................... can help you (Your father, Your Mother, God)
3.. on the LORD (Wait, Concentrate, Prey)

What does Proverbs 24:10 mean to you?

1...
2...

What changes will you make today because of this study?
1...
2...
3...

Personal Notes: Write whatever the Spirit of God lays in your heart, and pray about it

....
....
....
....
....
....
....
....
....
....
....
....
....
....
....
....
....
....
....
....

Assignment: Memorize. Isaiah 40:31
Bravo, you have completed Day 30. Now tick yourself a Pass

Today's Prayer

Lord Teach me to:

Today I am grateful for:

Epilogue:

In John 8:3-10, the Bible tells the story of the woman caught in adultery and brought to Jesus to be condemned. The Scribes, Pharisees, and the people had judged her. She ought to die according to the law of the land. But Jesus turned around and asked the one who had no sin to cast the first stone. In the end, all Jesus told her was he didn't condemn her, but she should go and sin no more.

God has a different opinion of you, regardless of what you are going through right now or the sentence you are serving. Although the system had condemned you, if you accept God's promises for you, God will not condemn you.

God foresaw the day when you would have to decide whether to follow men's paths and remain under the law and judgment of men, or to follow God's paths and obtain eternal freedom in the name of Jesus.

Jesus died to secure your eternal freedom, which is the greatest freedom you can ever know, even though you are currently behind bars.

You will be truly free if you accept Jesus today.

Say this Prayer."

Lord Jesus, I.. (put your name here) come to you by choice, and I place my faith in Jesus and what he did for me by dying in my place on the Cross of Calvary. I admit I have sinned against you and done many things I ought not to have done. I ask that you forgive and wash me with the blood of Jesus. Jesus, I ask you to come into my heart and purge my conscience of every guilt.

Thank you, Jesus, for making me a child of God and a new creation.

Amen

_____

Sign and date the above confession!

Prayer

Dear Jesus, it is because of your unwavering love that we, who were previously under the devil's control, are now free. However, Lord, there are those in this world, particularly those in prison, unaware of your unfailing love.

Jesus, I pray this book may impart the genuine gospel to the man who has just finished reading it, enabling him to recognize and accept your love for him, and therefore attain true freedom even while still incarcerated.

As the King of Kings and the Lord of Lords, I thank you and honor you. Father in heaven, it is extremely difficult for people who are entering prison for the first time.

Lord, comfort him and give him the strength to take each day as it comes. Let him learn to trust you as the God who comforts him as you see him through these trying times.

Even though he sinned against you, Lord, I know that you have pardoned him and that you will change his life for the better if he only puts his faith in you.

Please assist him in turning to you for solace, rather than to other things. Remind him of your love for him. I pray and believe in the name of Jesus. Amen.

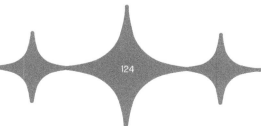

About the Author

"Every great dream begins with a dreamer. Always remember, you have within you the strength, the patience, and the passion to reach for the stars to change the world."–Harriet Tubman.

Annett Hill was born and raised by her grandparents on the beautiful island of Jamaica. After moving to New York City, she received an Associate's Degree in Office Administration at Plaza College and works as an Administrative Manager.

Annett has been passionate about healthy living and lifestyles since she lost weight, and is determined to share her experiences with others. She saw that there was an obesity epidemic in the Western World, and it would be difficult to approach people one-on-one. She wrote her first book, "How I lost 50 pounds without Exercise". She has since followed it up with more books on this topic to help as many people lose weight and be happier.

Later, Annett decided not only to help people with their physical health, but also with their spiritual health. She then started writing Christian books, which include "Daily Devotional for Black Men", "God's Promises for Life's Battles", "Daily Prayers", "God is Always on Time", "Promises from God for Dads", and "I am! God's Affirmations for Mom".

When she has time to relax, Annett loves going to the movies, baking, and listening to music. She also spends a lot of her time researching health and spiritual topics, to help her gain even more understanding of how she and her family, and others, can reap the benefits of healthy living.

She lives in Atlanta, Georgia today, with her husband and their son.

Also Available

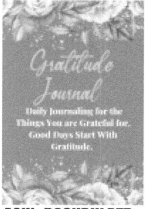  

ASIN: B08HBHLPTT   **ASIN: B09LGSH1Y4**   **ASIN: B09HFZCK6D**

ASIN: B08KHCRL6D   **ASIN: B08KHMQ6LK**   **ASIN: B08KH3TCY1**

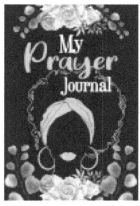  

ASIN: B08KHHVNB6   **ASIN: B08L8Z8JQ6**   **ASIN: B08GVLWCKL**

Made in the USA
Las Vegas, NV
23 January 2024

84758849R00075